Body Language:

How To Skillfully Connect, Attract, Influence And Read Anyone Undetected - Dominate ANY Situation

Table of Contents

Introduction

I want to thank you and congratulate you for downloading the book, Body Language: How To Skillfully Connect, Attract, Influence And Read Anyone Undetected - Dominate ANY Situation

Ever since you were born, you began to use body language to express yourself, on everything from needs to feelings. It is how we learn to get our needs met. As we age and learn to communicate with actual words, we continue to use a body language in our everyday communication, in order to have a need met, or show an emotion we are feeling that we are not yet able to express verbally.

You can greatly improve your chances of getting the response you want from others by simply understanding people better, as well as managing your own correct body signals that you are giving off. Communication is only about 7% verbal. Much of what is communicated is done some at an unconscious level.

You've heard that it's not what you say; but it's how you say it. Your whole body is communicating at all times. And there is an NLP presupposition that states, you cannot, not communicate. So, even though you or someone else may not have any sound coming out of their mouth, you can rest assured that we are always communicating something. How you communicate and understanding what is really being communicated to you is crucial to everything you do in your life. It can make the difference between landing a dream job or attracting that dream mate as well as many important areas of your life.

If you cannot pick up on the subtle nuances of non-verbal communication; you may be sending or receiving the wrong message. The more you use and learn this unconsciously spoken language the better you will become at decoding what's really being said to you underneath the words.

Reading Body Language is skill you anyone can master. It's used in all type of situations from therapy, to dating, to knowing whether or not your kids are telling you the truth. You will learn to fine-tune your senses of sight, hearing, and feeling ... and even gain intuition as you progress with learning body language.

Practice by simply watching people, in real life, on TV, or even YouTube. Work with the definitions of the variety of types of body language taught throughout this book and you will get better in over time.

I wish you lots of success!

Chapter 1: Reading Body Language

Body language is one of the main ways in which we recognize and identify a person's true feelings. Learning to read body language will help you to gain more insight into what another person is saying.

Unfortunately, not everyone is equipped with the ability to express themselves fully. Especially these days, with all the modern ways of communicating via texting and other quick messaging systems, people have become increasingly distant and to put it bluntly, not always 100% truthful. Learning to pick up on cues, gives you an extra tool that will come in handy more times, than not.

When learning to read body language, observation is the key. Focusing on what others say verbally is not always enough because our language capabilities are such that a person can say one thing and easily mean something else. People can have a tendency to use very vague language when expressing themselves. As you learn to closely observe, not only what is being said but, how it is said, you are developing the most essential skill require in order to successful read body language.

Other non-verbal cues such as facial expressions and tone of voice are also very important in learning to read body language. Observing facial expression is one of the easiest parts of the body to read, when it comes to learning to read body language. Though, it is very common that people will attempt to try to mask facial expressions. This very act of trying to conceal how they feel can then give a close observer the idea about how that person really feels about the topic that they are talking about.

You've done it yourself. You've tried to smile, when you really felt said. You've tried to put on a serious face, when you really felt like smiling. We've all been guilty of trying to change the expression on our faces. Now you will be able to pick up on this when others are doing it. And you will also know which other bodily cues to look at to get a better idea of what's really going on inside the mind of the person you're speaking with.

Believe it or not, learning to read body language is actually even be a more accurate than machines, which more often than not fail when it comes to recognizing human emotions.

Therefore, only another individual could develop the skill of being able to read body language that will act as a handy tool in many occasions. In your preparation to read body language, you'll be learning to focus on eye movements, other facial expressions, as well as many different things people do with their bodies when they are communicating. You're going to learn what is a defensive bodily posture versus one that is open. You'll be able to know when someone is evaluating you or trying to dominate you. You'll also get to know your own bodily postures and eye movements much better so you can send the right message.

In other words, although the language of the body works in general, not everyone who is crossing their arms is shut down. Sometimes, it just means that they are cold. Or it could mean that they are nervous and not completely ready to be open to you yet.

One of the best ways to get a person to your way of thinking, which is an advanced technique, is by modeling their bodily postures first ... get them into rapport with you, and once you know you are in sync, you can lead them through changing your expression or body posture ... that's right ... a person actually changes their psychology when they change their physiology.

A perfect example of this is ... try to recall a situation that makes you feel sad.

As you recall the situation, notice where your eyes are going ... notice where your head is going. Now ... do the opposite of that ... for example, if you were looking down when you recalled feeling bad, which is what is normal for most people, look up ... now while you are looking up ... try as hard as you can to feel bad. You just can't do it, can you.

I could go on to talk so much more about this, but then we'd never actually get to the reading and understanding of body language. So, let's get to the basics and then in another book I'll end up writing, we can go on to learn about more advanced techniques you can learn about rapport.

As you master the techniques of learning to read body language, you may just find yourself in your dream job, with your dream mate, driving to your dream home, in your dream home to plan your dream vacation. The possibilities are endless. In any case, having this skill is going to make your life easier by equipping you with the right tools to understand people around you.

Chapter 2: Understanding Body Language

Body language is a universal language. We all use body signs for non-verbal communication with others. The ability to understand body language is one of the most valuable tools you can possess in understanding others. When you understand what is really being communicated to you, it takes the conversation to a whole new level. You are able to make people feel at ease. You are easily able to establish a deep sense of rapport. You become likeable. All of these things are extremely useful to you because ultimately people like giving their love, support, business what have you to people that they like.

The bottom line: The more you understand another persons thoughts, feelings, needs, the more you can relay back to them what they need to get from you. The more you are able to relate to them, the more likeable you become. The more likeable you become, the more you are able to get what you want.

Understanding body language is not really difficult once you know the basics. It's sort of like learning a new language though, in that you are learning what different gestures and expression mean.

Understanding body language is used in many different professions. Usually, police officers are given some training in understanding body language as it is useful when interrogating a suspect or while talking to a witness. By using the other person's body language, the officer can easily determine whether the person is telling the truth.

Understanding body language is quite essential when it comes to the education profession. Especially with children, it is vital for teacher to have an understanding of body language.

Usually, kids are not fully capable of expressing their feelings using their vocabulary. Therefore, educators should have a basic understanding of body language in order to fully grasp what their students are trying to communicate.

When it comes to giving commands or conveying messages, understanding body language plays a key role. If the people with whom you work or interact with also have an understanding of body language, then it is quite easy for you to communicate with them. Additionally, the right combination of body language and verbal communication can produce more effective communication.

Understanding body language usually helps a person to portray her or his personality. There may be people you know of in your life that you've never actually had a conversation with, but you still can get a vague idea of how they operate based on watching their nonverbal expression. This is that energy vibration you pick up on, when you know someone is in a bad mood or a good mood. You feel it somehow without them saying a word.

But, it's due to the very fact that your subconscious mind already understands and interprets body language. And your subconscious mind sends you that information it knows through your feelings you get about another person. You don't' necessarily know on a conscious level why you feel the way you about them, but you know, there's just something about them that you either want to experience more of or that you want to avoid being around.

Chapter 3: Interpreting Body Language From Head To Toe

Body language interpretation involves the study of gestures, actions and facial expressions related to human behaviour.

In our daily lives, the art of proper body language interpretation is all about the ability to look closely at the individual you are communicating with and picking up various signals, some of the basic ones of which we have already described. . A key factor of body language interpretation is to ensure that you are subtle about what you are doing so that the other person does not realize what you are doing this. Failure to do so will result in the person feeling uncomfortable and distracted by your behaviour.

Body language entails gestures and movements involving all different parts of the body, from head to toe. We're going to go over the basic meanings of each area of the body. In later chapters, we will decipher the different body language meanings in order by mood or attitude. Each signal of body language may have different meanings, depending on the situation in which it was delivered.

As an aside, before delving too deeply into the gestures your body speaks, many of these are going to seem like very common knowledge. Some will not. The gestures will apply to many people, and will have a different meaning when others do them. The point is that there are many things to look for and the better you get at A) Knowing what to look for but B) and most importantly, knowing the person who's making the gestures, you will figure out what the gestures mean to them the better you know them. You will even pick up on unique gestures not covered in this book and those are just as important to notice and make a mental note of. Also, keep in mind, this book is being written in Northern America. These gestures are typical of Americans and may translate differently or have entirely different meanings in other cultures or countries.

Try to use these as a general reference to help you to pay attention and sharpen your ability to look at people in a different way.

Head

You can signal yes or no by the movement of your head. Nodding usually means yes or I agree. When you have someone nodding their head in agreement, you know you are in good rapport with them and they like what you have to say.

Tilting the head backwards or to the side indicates that the person is thinking deeply or considering another thought or idea.

Face

Facial expressions are obvious visible signs of how someone truly feels, however there are some people who have practiced and become very good at controlling their facial expressions and they may come across on the surface as somewhat expressionless or passive.

This might be a warning sign. When someone is trying to hide their expression or how they feel, they may be trying to deceive you somehow. Either that or for some reason they are very uncomfortable expressing their feelings. It doesn't necessarily mean that they are dishonest, but if you are say, trying to form a relationship with this person, it might mean that you have to work hard at getting them to share themselves openly with you.

Eyes

Cliché as it is, the eyes are indeed the windows of the soul. The eye body language is one of the most powerful mediums of nonverbal communication. It can either support or betray whatever you are saying. Even the slightest movement of the eye can indicate the biggest meaning.

Even with an inexpressive face, nobody could miss what is being expressed through the eyes. The eyes can speak volumes in most cases.

Eye Contact

During a conversation, it is normal to have eye contact. It means different things in different situations.

Eye Contact is generally a strong indication that you have someone's complete attention and interest. It can also mean honesty. And depending on the situation, it can be an indication of attraction. You can determine if somebody is lying to you because it's nearly impossible for them to maintain eye contact with you for very long when they are lying. There is a physiological reason for this actually. The eyes have a tendency to look in a particular direction when a person is making up stories.

If the person's eyes are not completely focused on you, it can be an indication of several things and you will need to dig a little deeper to figure out the exact meaning in that particular situation. Typically it would mean that he or she is not interested in the conversation. But, it isn't necessarily true in 100% of the cases. It may also indicate doubt, suspicion, or lack of trust. It could even mean that the person is terribly attracted to you and they are too shy to let you see their eyes, which might give them away. They could also simply be distracted.

Appropriate use of eye contact also includes when to break eye contact. A long eye contact has many interpretations. It may mean a focused attention or sign of attraction. But this can sometimes be uncomfortable, thus the trick is to just look at the bridge of the nose.

Long eye contact may also indicate a sign of authority or domination if one can do it without much blinking. However, prolonged eye contact may also pose as a threat, so breaking it from now and then is essential. But breaking it may indicate other meanings as well, such as situations wherein one wants to end the conversation, has been insulted or found out, or is being threatened.

Eye Movements

If the person has dilated pupils, he or she is interested in the conversation.

The eyes looking in different directions also have different meanings. When one looks up to the right, it means that he is imagining visual images. Meanwhile, when he looks up to the left direction, it means that he is trying to recall a memory. However, there are still instances where it is in a reversed order, depending on the person. Try to test him first by asking him to recall a known memory and to picture out an event.

On the other hand, looking down may mean that one is talking to himself, but this is more evident if there is also movement of the lips. It is also a potential signal of shame, guilt or submission. When people look down, it typically means that they are accessing how they felt about something. Looking down on another person means that he is control of the situation or is talking to someone who is under his superiority.

Lateral eye movements can indicate signs of dishonesty, distraction, or it could be that that are recalling auditory information. When looking from one eye to the other then going up to the forehead, it means that you are looking at somebody with superiority. When going down to the nose, you are talking to someone within the level of your status. And when looking from one eye to the other and down to the lips, it indicates a sign of attraction or romance.

Eyes Expressions

Different emotions and mood can be expressed through gazing, glancing, winking, squinting, closing, and staring. Gazing indicates interest or concentration. Glancing indicates desire. For example, one glances at food. It means that has a desire to eat. Winking indicates an agreement, and it could also be a means of flirtation. A person would squint his eyes if he were uncertain or trying to evaluate or verify truthfulness. Closing the eyes means that the person wants a moment to be away from the world, or simply trying to remember. And lastly, staring indicates a state of shock, surprise or disbelief.

Eyes of Romance and Flirtation

Eyes can show affection to another person. Winking is a way people flirt. The process of looking at someone, quickly looking away, and then staring back is an obvious indication of attraction. A lingering, warm gaze is also an indicator of romance or desire.

If you know how to read and understand eye language, you will know what the person you are conversing with wants or doesn't want. And, if you know how to properly use it, you can take control of any situation or know the proper timing to use different eye movements or expressions.

The eyes are also used in flirting, especially in knowing if the person is attracted to you or not. When your eyes meet across the room, and then one of you looks away, and then looks back, it is a signal of attraction. Another signal of attraction happens when the eyes go down to the lips and then back to the eyes again.

If the eyes look up to the forehead of another person, it means he is talking to someone with superiority. When the eye goes down to the nose, it means that there are no figures of authority in between both parties.

Again, these signs tell you what to look for. But, you really do need to spend time getting to know what is normal for that person in most cases in order to truly know for sure wheat these signs mean for them.

Eyebrows

Raised eyebrows express surprise or shock. A flick of the eyebrows while glancing at another individual shows that the person is acknowledging the other person or greeting him or her

Nose

Touching or rubbing the nose is one of the most common self-touching gestures, which is usually done by people who are lying or trying to hide something.

Lips

Licking or biting the lips is one of the typical signals of flirting by women.

A kissing is a gesture can be done to show one's affection, and also used as a form of greeting.

Shoulders and Back

When the shoulders are squared and pulled back, but without too much tightening of the back muscles, that indicates confidence.

When the back muscles are rigid and stiff, this indicates tension and nervousness. Slouching of the back or shoulders signifies laziness or boredom.

Arms And Hands

The arms and hands are another big key to body language interpretation.

- An open position of the arms portrays a feeling of honesty and that the person is accepting the situation.
- Crossing the arms signifies a defensive posture, and it may also mean doubt or suspicion of what the other person is saying.
- Open hand palms express a feeling of being relaxed and comfortable.
- Putting the hands in the pockets is generally a sign of nervousness or lack of interest.
- The hands on the waist may indicate anger or fury.

- Another common hand gesture is the clenched fist. This indicates anger, frustration, defensiveness, resistance, or confidence
- The way a person shakes hands can have all kinds of meanings:
- It's customary to stand up to shake hands. This shows a sign of respect. Eye contact held throughout the length of the handshake is a sign of sincerity.
- The person who initiates the handshake is showing a sign of confidence, while sweaty palms indicates anxiousness or nervousness.
- A Firm handshake with the hand pointing downward is universally recognized as a sign of confidence. The palms should also come in contact with each other. Too tight, it may mean they are overcompensating for something. On the other hand, a weak handshake with the hand pointing upward indicates shyness or nervousness.

Legs And Feet

If the person's legs are shoulder width apart, either when standing or in a seated position, it indicates that the person is relaxed.

Crossed legs when standing may indicate shyness.

Crossing the legs when seated is something most people do purely for comfort, especially women. But, sometimes it can mean that the person is feeling defensive or withdrawn or closed off.

Foot position is also a useful tool in body language interpretation. If the feet of the person are pointing at you when you are standing opposite one another, this indicates that the person is at ease with you. Their eyes will be focused on you and their head will be pointed in your direction.

However, if the person's feet are pointing in away from you, it is very likely that their head and eyes will also not be on you. This may indicate a lack of interest or a feeling of discomfort or awkwardness.

These are just a few of the tips that can be used for body language interpretation. Body language interpretation is a useful skill that you need to work on regularly. It is extremely beneficial if you know how to decipher the meanings of another person's body language. However, the indications are not true at all times. Not all impressions from reading body language last. This will only be supportive if you already have an idea on the personality of the person.

With more practice, you will be better and subtler in your approach.

Misinterpreting Body Language

These are general of course. Just like dreams don't always have the same meaning to everyone. The ability to read someone's body gestures is sometimes not completely reliable. The gestures performed by one person that may be considered rude for example, may be just an innocent habit of another person. As you get to know a person better, you will learn their unique body language.

Chapter 4: How To Use Your Own Body Language

As we've mentioned, body language is a form of nonverbal communication wherein one can send or receive messages through body movements, gestures, facial expression, and the like. There are general acts of body language that almost everyone does in his or her daily life. However, do you know how to speak this language? Can you understand other people just by reading their body language? The importance of knowing how to speak through body language is that you now have the ability to have more control over the conversations you have with people, by picking up on their non- verbal cues, and using your own to send them messages that generally go undetected by their conscious mind.

Personal Space

Each of us has his or her own personal space. It is somewhat like a comfort zone. It is an invisible region that surrounds you, and if someone tries to invade it, you feel uncomfortable or threatened. But one's personal space is dependent on certain situations. A person who grew up in the city with crowded streets has a smaller personal space compared to one who lives in the rural area. Learning how to respect one's personal space is one method to make communication through body language more effective between two or more people. Body movements and gestures are better received and understood when there is an appropriate distance.

Body Gestures And Movements

Various body parts are used in the body language As we have already discussed, your hands, arms, legs, head, and body posture are communicating different things which people pick up on unconsciously. When you understand the signals you are sending by using the different gestures we already discussed, you are expressing yourself. For example, if you want to let another person know you are interested in him or her, or in the conversation in general, keep your hands open and that will show them you are open to them. If you try to hide your hands from him, like putting them into your pockets, they are going to subconsciously feel like either you are hiding something from them or you are already getting bored. Put your palm upward or outward and show them that you are comfortable and interested. Also, leaning your body or directing it towards that person is also another signal that you are listening.

You can still give a good impression even in the tensest situations, like in a job interview. You simply avoid gestures that are giving off signals that you are nervous, uncomfortable, or anxious. These signals would be slouching fidgeting, drumming your fingers, shuffling your feet, or trembling. These actions portray a lack of confidence.

You can also speak through handshakes. A firm one with the palm pointing downwards and arm slightly extended indicates confidence or power. Meanwhile, a weak handshake pointing upward is an indication of tension or shyness.

You must also be aware of the message you are trying to convey whenever you cross your arms. This is one of the actions that you must avoid. This will tell another person that you might be hiding something, lying, or being impatient.

Let Your Eyes Do the Talking

Your eyes can clearly express what you feel or desire. Eye contact is the most important element of body language since it could mean so many positive things such as interest, confidence, eagerness to listen, and sincerity. The inability to hold long eye contact can indicate dishonesty or discomfort.

When you learn how to speak using your body, you are going to find a much easy delivering your message than words alone could ever do. It is very useful in leaving the kind of impression you want to create in almost all situations. One caveat however, is to keep in mind that not everyone interprets body language the same way ... many of these typical rules are very general ... you will learn through experience and fine tuning your awareness of how people are responding to you.

Chapter 5: Types of Body Language

In this chapter, you will learn many types of body language. Two of the most common types of body language people can easily pick up on are romantic body language and greeting body language. Other forms of body language you will discover are aggressive, attentive, bored, closed, deceptive, defensive, dominant, emotional, evaluating, open, power, ready, relaxed, and submissive.

We will look at each category listed alphabetically, and explain signals to look for in each

Aggressive Body Language

Aggressive body language is way more then simply being punched in the face or punching someone. There are many types of aggressive signals that if picked up on early can save you from being a receiver of a physical attack or give you time to turn the aggression down. Aggressive body language is a signal to a possible physical threat or a verbal threat at the least. Physical confrontations can never lead to anything good so learning to pick up the threat signals early on is extremely beneficial. If you work in a setting where there are volatile people, prison settings for example, knowing signals of aggressiveness could even save your life.

Aggressive body language can come from in many different forms. Facial signals that can alert you to a possible threat are frowns, pursed lips, reddening of face, a sneer look, clinched jaw, stare downs with a squint, and jerking of the head toward you much like one would jerk their body towards you in an aggressive advancement.

Another common facial threat signal is a person getting right up in your face with their face. With all of these gestures, it is best you step back a couple feet to put a bit of distance between you and the aggressive person to give you a chance to possibly defuse the situation. The attack stance of body language is typically the positioning of feet for stability, and clinching of fist and muscles. Some may even get a bit bouncy with their feet, like a boxer.

However, this is the typical, there are some people that really show little outward physical cues that indicate they are about to punch you. People who present with a flat affect may show very little to no indication that they are about to physically attack another. This is when body language alone can put one in a risky situation and it is important to listen to word cues as well.

Another form of aggressive body language is crossing ones personal space, mental or emotional boundaries. Everyone has a comfort zone called his or her personal space.

When that is crossed physically (e.g. getting up in someone's face, bumping into them, physically touching another without permission etc.) that invasion of space can be very upsetting for some people and may even be looked upon as an aggressive body language move. People who do this maybe be very well intentioned, but they may also be trying to get into close proximity, so they can have power over another by making them feel uncomfortable and to make it easier for them to get physical.

Aggressive body language gestures are indicator that you may be at risk. Hand gestures are often used to provoke another into a physical confrontation. For example, "flipping someone off", gang signs, or thrusting of the arms and these are generally followed by verbal insults. Another obvious great indicator is slamming things, fist on table, the wall, the door, etc.). Kicking and Stomping are yet a couple of other ways to display aggressive body language, without actually making physical contact.

Attentive Body Language

Attentive body language is the act of showing through body language that you are listening and hearing what another is saying. Yawning or nodding off would be an example of inattentive body language. Being able to properly exhibit attentive body language can make a huge impact if you are applying for a job, or are in any field of employment that requires verbal contact with people.

Another situation where having great skills in attentive body language is in personal relationships and intimate situations. Strong attentive body language shows that you have a sincere interest in what another is saying, is flattering, and will most likely result in mutual attention.

One way to appear to be actively listening to another through body language is by leaning into the person who is talking, however, respect personal boundaries when doing so. You will be able to tell if a person is listening to you attentively if their gaze is on you and does not go off in other directions sporadically during the conversation.

They will also blink less then normal. Often times when a person is attentively listening to another their frown line will be indented showing that they are concentrating on what you are saying. You will notice a nodding of the head in agreement or disagreement of things you are saying along with verbal utterances such as "hmmm, uh huh, of mmm". The person listening may also mimic your body language. This is a great way to tell that you are in sync.

Closed Body Language

Have you ever wondered if your spouse, friend, co-worker, or boss was bored with everything that came out of your mouth, but you were not quite able to tell by their body language? Well now, you will be able to tell if what you are saying is falling upon deaf ears. One of the first cues that someone is totally tuning you out is their gaze level. If they are constantly distracted by every little noise or movement you can bet they are not truly paying attention to you, regardless of how many times they tell you they are listening.

Watch for frigidity hands, feet, twitching eyes, all of these are indicators that you do not have their full attention. A huge clue is when a person begins to yawn or slouch. Granted, yawning is can be an indicator that a person is lacking oxygen, however, when bored, a person will also yawn. If someone straight up falls asleep on you, then you have a real problem with your presentation skills and should consider taking some speech or affective communication classes. Some reasons people may choose to tune out is that the topic you are discussing with them is something they either don not understand or do not want to understand. Or maybe it's something they have heard you say repeatedly.

If a person has no stake in what you are discussing, it is very easy for them to lose interest and become bored quickly. When speaking to a group or on a one on one basis.

it is important to use body language while you speak. Facial, and hand movements can help to emphasize what you are trying to get across as well as stimulate both the visual and auditory senses of your audience. Long drawn out explanations is another quick way to lose the attention. of your audience

Keep it short and to the point. You do not need to re-explain the same thing 50 different ways to get your point across. Always ask question whenever speaking with anyone. It will be a good indicator of their interest level as well if they understand the message you are trying to convey.

Often, if a person is bored you may also see closed body language. Closed body language tells you that your audience has totally shut down and as far as they are concerned, you are not even in the same room with them any longer even if you are standing directly in front of them. Teenagers can demonstrate this perfectly sometimes. Closed body language can also present a defensive action for people as well. If you are confronting a person and they exhibit closed body language, it may be because you are scaring them and in order for you to get across what you are trying to say effectively, you should change your approach.

Examples of closed body language are curling up in a ball, rocking, tightly folded arms, tightly crossed legs, and a downward gaze or fixated gaze at an object, such a wall, or even the floor or feet. There may be many reason why you receive closed body language from an individual. Do not automatically assume it is because of you or what you are saying.

The person may have just had an extremely difficult day. When you experience someone who appears to close up during a discussion, notice what was being said at the time that the body language changed. It can be a good indicator as to what is possibly going on with them.

When a person feels threatened, even verbally, their body will react. They will get into either a defensive mode or an aggressive mode. In the defensive mode, it is a self-preservation mode. Curling up in a ball protects vulnerable organs and body parts in case of an attack. It can also act as a self-nurturing affect, to sooth a person.

Another reason people may exhibit closed body language is that they are trying to hide something from the other person such as tears or facial expressions. Ways to move a person from closed body language to a more open and accepting body language is to offer them something to hold such as a drink, or with a child, you can provide a toy. Another way is to mimic their body language, however not in a demeaning way, but in a way that shows them unconsciously you are like them. This will help establish rapport. Once you have gotten into rapport, you can move them into a more open body position by leading them with your body becoming open again.

Deceptive Body Language

Deceptive body language should be necessary for everyone to learn. It can help you to distinguish if someone is being honest with you or trying to pull a fast one. Mind you, there are those that are quite good at covering deceptive body language, such as sales people, psychopaths, and criminally minded individuals. One common way to tell if a person is being deceptive by their body language is to watch for anxiety cues. Some common anxiety cues are sweating, tension, rubbing the back of the neck or other body parts, sudden movements, body twitches, change in vocal tone or inflection, increase in rate of speech, chewing on the inside of the mouth, and putting the hands in the pockets or having fidgety hands.

A person, when lying, will often times try to hide their deception by attempting to gain control over their body language through forced smiles and exaggerated hand gestures. You see, the body does not lie. And people intuitively know this. This may come out as odd clumsy or jerky movements. Their speech may become hesitant in their attempt to slow it down and think intensively about what to say next. They will often speak looking distracted and avoid eye contact. If standing, they may shift their weight from one foot to another more often then normal.

Law enforcement is trained to read body language. As part of that training, they learn about how the brain works and how the body reacts when using different parts of brain when thinking, such as eye movement. It is believed that the direction one looks when responding to a question can help in determining if the person is lying. This is not always a good indicator to be used in truth finding; however, if a person looks to the right while answering a question, you should at least pay close attention to what they are saying.

Here's why. It is thought to be an instinctive action to look to the right when one is utilizing the left side of their brain, the logic and analytic side and to look to the left when using the right side of your brain, the emotional and creative side. It is thought that when a person lying they utilize the left part of their brain to create the lie which causes their eyes to gaze to the right. There is documentation that states differing views on lying and eye gaze, some say a person is lying when they look to the right, because they are using the creative side of their brain to make up the story, where others say the left, because they are trying to use logic to make the lie make sense to themselves. Another theory is that in either case, it is reversed for left-handed people.

So do not be judge and jury just because of the direction a person looks when they respond to a question you ask or when they are telling you a story. Pay close attention to all their body language, as well as their words before throwing the book at someone.

This information is going to come in handy more when you are able to pick up on and remember the direction of the eyes in the case of someone telling a lie. You can easily calibrate for this by asking them a set of test questions and then asking them to purposely lie about something and watch where their eyes go.

Here are a few more interesting things about eye gaze when trying to recall a memory or store data. When we are trying to recall a memory, we use the right side of our brain, making our eyes gaze to the left. When you are seeking visual memories your eyes gaze upward, and when a person gazes downward, they are trying to recall emotional memories. However, eyes gazing right to left means they are trying to recall or process auditory memories.

Observing body language can be handy. Especially if the other person is not telling the truth. Body language when lying differs and can easily be picked up by anyone who is observant.

Body language when lying often goes unnoticed. However, it is one of the easiest ways to know if someone is lying to you. Smiles are one of the easiest body language signs to read. People who smile for the sake of it, generally use only the muscles around the mouth.

A real smile uses more muscles and the cheeks of a person normally move when smiling. A person who is hiding something from you will avoid making eye contact. This is because the eyes are an essential component of reading a person's body language. Eyes often reveal whether is person is lying or not.

It is extremely difficult for a person to lie and maintain a straight face. People who are lying often look around and constantly keep shifting the position of their eyes. This is common body language when lying. If you are in such a situation you are probably being lied to.

A person who is lying easily becomes defensive. This is one of the most common things they do ... or they may raise their voice or change their tone.

A person who is lying will often have to fake real body language gestures. An example of this would be when acting surprised. The person may have a latent reaction and not act spontaneously.

Because people who are lying will change the tone of their voice, if someone says I love you, but they are using a tone that is extremely different for them, they are probably feeling very ill at ease about saying it, and it might mean they are not telling you the truth.

Some people become stiff when lying. Also, they usually use their hands to cover their face by scratching their nose or covering their mouth while speaking.

Often times, Lying is used when flirting. People will lie to try to make themselves more likeable. Watch for sudden changes or shifts in their body. Being alert to these changes will enable you to know when someone is providing you with false information. Observing hand movements is also handy. Lairs often twitch their fingers or play with their hair.

Just keep in mind ... when what is being spoken is not the truth, the body cannot lie. It is totally incongruent and uncomfortable to lie and the body will let you know by demonstrating a shift in how they are handling themselves physically. Being observant of their body movements when they are not lying and when they are lying is going to dramatically help you to know if you are being lied to.

Defensive Body Language

When a person is feeling defensive, their body language shows this in a few different ways. Feeling defensive means that the person feels threatened or under some sort of attack ... The body goes into fight or flight response mode. Even though there may be no real physical threat actually occurring, they may be feeling emotionally threatened or mentally threatened.

Automatically when a person feels like they are being attacked, they want to protect themselves from being hurt.

They will try to put a barrier between them self and the person or situation that is making them feel uncomfortable. This could be a chair, a table, or even holding a package out in front of them making an obstacle between them self and the perceived threat. They may grip their keys in between their fingers. They may cross their arms. Another defensive body posture cue is when someone becomes extremely stiff or rigid.

On the opposite end of the spectrum, a person in a defensive mode may look around, trying to find a way to escape. They may even run away. Hence the term fight or flight response. This is a natural response most people feel when they have any feeling of stress, tension or anxiety and feeling defensive or under attack, is definitely one way to provoke such a response and the ensuing body language.

Dominant Body Language

Dominant body language is closely related to aggressive body language but at a lesser emotional level. The ultimate goal of dominant body language is to demonstrate power over another, but not necessarily in an aggressive manner, more so in an authoritative manner. A person demonstrating dominant body language will often try to make their body appear larger then what it really is.

Often times they will cross their arms with their hands under their biceps in an attempt to push their chest out more giving them a larger appearance. Men and women will hold their hands on their hips with elbows out wide while standing chest out and chin up. You will see many mothers in this position when disciplining their children.

A great example of using dominant body language over another is a detective interrogating a suspect in an interrogation room.

Think back to a scene in a movie where there is a suspect in an interrogation room. You will recall from the scene that, the detective is usually standing making the suspect sit to given him a dominating height over the suspect

Pacing back and forth may be used ... and this is, much like marking his territory.

By invading the personal space someone, they make the person feel uncomfortable, especially with the added height and being talked down to.

You will also see facial expression to taunt, control, and dominate the situation. It can be in the form of stare downs, rolling of the eyes, yawning, squinting the eyes, or smirking.

Emotions and Body Language

Emotions body language is a very broad area as a person feels many different emotions. Anger, for instance, appears different from happy body language. However some body language signals of happy can be mixed with sad body language.

There are many non-verbal signs that can help you to determine what another person is feeling emotionally, however they are not exclusive and no two people necessarily react the same way to the same stimuli. What you might think would make a person sad, may actually have no impact on them at all. Conversely, you may think a person will not have any reaction, only to discover that they respond very dramatically.

Starting with anger, a person can be angry, for many reasons, from getting a bad test score, having bad day at work, a bounced check, an argument and many other situations. Some things may anger one person deeper then another. Common body language signals of anger are: a flushed face or neck, clenched jaw or fist, pacing, invasion of personal space, and the use of the aggressive body language, we talked about earlier.

The emotions of fear, anxiety, or nervousness are all part of the same set of emotions and therefore they have similar characteristics when it comes to body language. Knowing a bit about the situation while reading the persons body language will you to gain further insight into exactly which of these emotions they are experiencing; fear, anxiety, or nervousness. The body language of these emotions can present itself as the body breaking out in a cold sweat, having a pale face, getting a dry mouth, diverting from eye contact, or they can appear as though they are on the verge of tears with damp eyes.

They may also exhibit a trembling lip, twitching of the eye, voice tremors, stuttering, cracks in the voice, sweating, heightened pulse, clenched fist, muscles, or jaw. Also, people forget to breathe when they are experiencing these emotions, so you may notice extended periods of holding their breath. Some people may get fidgety while others may take on more of a defensive body language stance. As you can see, many of these body language signals are present in other emotions we've talked about.

Reading the body, is not the same as mind reading. It's going to give you some of the story, but not the entire story. So, if you know a little more about what is going on, you can generally determine whether they are nervous, fearful, or anxious.

Sadness generally presents it's as slouching or drooping of the shoulders or the body going limp, possibly the lip will tremble too. Of course, tears are a pretty obvious sign of sadness; unless of course they are laughing so hard it makes them cry. A person, who is sad, will generally speak with a monotone voice.

Embarrassment can appear as a red face, avoidance of eye contact, a grimace, or a meek smile.

Embarrassment can also cause withdrawal in some people.

Surprised body language will cause a widening of the eyes and raised eyebrows. Their mouth may drop open and even appear startled or make a sudden movement back.

Happiness. The eyes will be wide open. can show as tears of joy, a true smiling mouth and eyes, and an overall relaxed demur.

Extreme happiness may cause a person to the happy dance where they are jumping around flailing their arms around or clapping wildly.

Although all of these are very common types of body language used to express an emotion, there are those people who are not as expressive and may not present any of these exaggerated expression. They could be extremely happy and only have a slight smile if that.

The key to reading body language is to become very observant of what someone does in their different states and then you will know when they are in that state by watching them and without them saying a word.

Relaxed / Open Body Language

Relaxed or Open body language generally expresses comfort.

Open arms and open hand palms are the biggest signs of comfort. Especially when the hands are lying loosely in their lap or just looking rested in general. This expresses the persons desire to fully disclose themselves. They are relaxed in their current situation. If a person was exhibiting closed body language and suddenly you realize that it changes to open, notice what it was that you may have said or done that caused them to become open toward you. Of course the reverse is also true.

Here are some other signs to look for: Facial expression is relaxed with a possible slight smile or relaxed mouth. Their legs are uncrossed and parallel.

Their eyes are gazing and making prolonged eye contact with you. They are smiling. Sitting up straight or leaning back comfortably A persons breathing is slower than normal and steady.

The whole body is relaxed without any signs of tension or muscle tone. Even their skin tone color will be normal, not too pale, not too flush.

You will also notice that a person's feet point toward a person that they feel comfortable with and away from someone they do not.

Learn to determine quickly what was said that possibly caused them to open up or close down so you can direct the conversation in such a way that creates the same type of feeling in the future.

Power Body Language

Power body language is a form of dominant body language. People who use power body language on a regular basis are those who are in a position of authority or like to act as if they are. It can be a spouse or a partner that tries to retain the power in a relationship using power body language. If a person appears to always have control over you, they are more then likely exhibiting a lot of power body language, and it is one way they have achieved power over you.

In the business world power is exhibited and acknowledge by the employees starting from the company parking lot. Those in positions of power always have the reserved and best parking spots.

This is a way of exhibiting ones power and status over another. They display their position and status from the car they drive to the size of the office where they work, with a door that they can open or close to allow them the power to select when or if they choose to deal with their subordinates.

Power handshakes are one way a person will demonstrate their power over another. Upon greeting someone they feel is of lesser status then they are, the power person may give an excessively firm grip in their handshake.

A person using power body language will hold a gaze longer then normal, another way of saying, I am powerful. It's just enough to make the receiver squirm a bit.

If it makes you feel uncomfortable as someone who is on the receiving end of this, you can easily break the gaze.

Another move used to establish who has the power is the person will dictate where another will sit, either by pulling out a chair for you or gesture toward where you should sit.

Knowing this, if you want to be the one establishing the power, you can just as easily be the one in charge. When you are going meeting a person, be prepared, get there early and get your seat first. Plan to seat yourself facing out, and them facing you where there are the least amount of distractions. That way you will be sure to have their undivided attention.

Submissive Body Language

A person who is submissive is trying to protect him or herself from coming across as aggressive or as a threat. They are doing whatever they can in their power to avoid confrontation.

These are a few of the positions a person who feels submissive will take on: A crouching position, even slightly with knees slightly bent.

Hunching inwards reduces the size of the body, limiting the potential of being hit also protecting vital areas.

Arms are held in.

Putting the body in a lower position shows the other person that you are not a physical threat.

Even in sitting, a submissive person will choose a lower chair or slump in order to be lower that others.

Staying perfectly still, Keeping the head down, turning the chin and head down protects the vulnerable neck from attack.

The eyes will be wide and attentive, showing the person you are respecting what they are saying.

Submissive people smile more at dominant people, but they are not usually a genuine smile that would be with the whole face .. only the mouth moves.

When the submissive person moves, they make small movement. Women tend to exhibit more submissive body language then men.

Chapter 6: Romantic Body Language

Romance And Signs of Attraction

Your eyes, facial expressions, and body movements can truly express whether or not you want to engage in a romantic or intimate relationship with another person.

What The Eyes Could Say

The eyes are strong indicators of romance and attraction. They can express, flirt, and even seduce much better than words. Eye contact may not mean anything if it only happens briefly. But once it lasts longer and with an intense look, he or she is probably into you. Winking will also work, but it does require the right timing.

Smile And Facial Expressions

The smile is one of the greatest signs that he or she likes you. It means that he is truly interested, comfortable, and enjoying. But make sure you know how to determine a forced smile from a sincere one. Raising the eyebrows, although unconsciously done, has also been observed to be done by people flirting with each other.

Magic Of Touch

Sometimes, leaning towards another is just not enough. Closing the distance is much better. A light tap or stroking of the arm could send electric signals to another person. Some people might make up a reason to touch someone, like having a smudge on their face or a something on their shirt .

Difference Between Men And Women

Compared to men, women can send signals of attraction five times stronger. They are more flirtatious than men and most of this flirting is done intentionally. They love to play with their hair, tossing the hair over the shoulder, and play something with their hands such as a wine glass. Most women are also quite good in seduction and teasing men, especially when they involve their lips. Biting and licking their lips, putting on lipstick, eating or drinking slowly are the usual moves of an interested woman.

Meanwhile, men usually try to appear masculine to show their prowess to the women they like by giving them a look at the full length of their body. They try to stand taller and square off their shoulders. They also unconsciously touch their ties or collar, and this means they find you irresistible.

Signals Of An Invitation

You would determine if a person likes you if he or she would give the following signs: prolonged aye contact, raising of eyebrows, smiling back, laughing with you, leaning, closing the distance, imitation of actions of the partner, touching, preening, and the like. If you received these signs, it means there is a big possibility that you could take your interaction to a higher level.

Signs Indicating No

A person is most likely not interested when he or she never glances back at you. You can also determine that person is starting to get bored or uninterested in you when his or her eyes start to wander, sigh, yawn, have a passive or neutral facial expression, and the like.

The signals of body language in terms of romance and attraction are easy to detect if you know how to interpret one's actions. Understanding gestures and body movements of another person can definitely help you know in advance if you can be intimate together or be rejected.

Signs Of Falling In Love

How can you tell that a person is already falling in love with you? A person's body language can spell out his or her true feelings and intentions for you. A person in love has that certain glow every time he or she is with that special person, but what are the other signs?

You will notice that a person is already falling for you if he can't stand being far from you, gives more smiles and laughter, mirrors your actions, cannot keep his eyes off you, and has that certain glow.

Personal Space And Distance

A person in love with you finds several ways just to be closer to you. You will know that a person's personal space has gotten smaller when he or she gets comfortable with you even in the slightest distance. And notice if in a room full of people, he will always longs to be closer to you.

That person would also tend to lean their body towards you, whether when sitting down or standing up. The direction of his or her body would always be turned towards you.

More Touch, Smiles, And Laughter

A person who is starting to fall for you will be completely mesmerized by what you have to say, thus they give more reactions than he or she did during your first dates. There would be more laughter even at the cheesiest jokes. While talking, one will find difficult to keep from smiling, especially during silence. This is because that person is truly enjoying his or her time with you.

He or she would also touch you from time to time. A tap on the shoulder, placing the hand on the small of the back, hugging, and holding the hands are some of the most common touching body language in falling in love.

The Mirroring Actions

This is a funny yet very sweet signal of attraction since it is done unconsciously most of the time. This is where a person imitates the actions of that special person. For example, you will prop your chin onto your hand, the person in love with you will follow that same action. This is done because you are in literally sync with each other.

The Longer Stare

A person in love with you simply cannot take their eyes off you. Especially when the feelings are new and just beginning to develop, he or she will find difficulty in concentrating on other things. The stare is usually intimate or intense, and it is accompanied with a slight smile.

That Certain Glow

Somehow unexplainable, a person has a certain aura around him or her when he or she is in love and happy. It is due to the extreme happiness and joy coming from the inside, and this is well reflected with a sparkle in the eyes and a smile that is hard to remove from the face.

When a person falls in love, it changes him entirely and this is reflected in his or her body language. Some people fail to notice this, but these signs are definitely there. The person himself is even unaware that he is already providing hints and clues about his true feelings for that special someone. Most people find them hard to miss, and would love these signals of deep attraction sent through the silence but delivered by simple romantic actions and gestures.

Many of these signs I have mentioned are pretty obvious. I mention them because these signs MUST be present in order for you to believe someone is falling in love or even attracted to you.

In the absence of the above signs, it's probably just wishful thinking. So, look for the above and the following key signs more as a validation that what you are thinking is actually happening.

The Body Language Of Men

Men are indeed much more difficult to read compared to women. It is because they are less expressive and have reserved facial expressions. Fact is you cannot know a man well enough without interaction for a period of time. But here are some tips on the interpretations on the typical acts of male

41

body language. By understanding men, you will know when he is flirting. In the end, you may find men's behavior less difficult to read.

Typical Acts Of Men

Men are less expressive than women. It is rare that a man's face will truly brighten, the same way a woman's does. But nonetheless, you can always see in their eyes, which are never dull when they are interested in something or someone. A man will also tend to tilt his head during a conversation. Men also tend to be less able to remain still then the typical woman, so you may notice them having to readjust themselves more often. You may think they are feeling uneasy or nervous, but this is just typical movement for men, whereas women can remain perfectly still for long periods of time.

Some Signs That He's Attracted To You

Men's flirting actions are not as obvious as compared to women. But when he is looking at you with a certain brightness accompanied with a smile, he definitely is into you. Raising the eyebrows is a flirting signal as well, but also be sure to observe if he raises his eyebrows at just anyone or only at you. Men also like to come in to close the distance between himself and a woman he likes. You will find him leaning forward and maybe even whispering in your ear just to be closer.

Bottom line is, look for ways in which the man treats you uniquely different than how he is treating other people. If you notice that he is acting different toward you, he is probably attracted to you. However, do not misinterpret a man's sweet and tender actions for a fact that he is definitely into you. He may be just a flirtation guy in general.

These are just clues. The biggest sign that they are into you is that they will tell you. Most men are not shy about revealing their intentions to a women they like.

A few more subtle signs to look for if you want to try to predict whether he's interested in your or not are:

His lips will part slightly the moment he sees you.

He will be inclined to touch something on his person, his necktie, he chest, his pocket, something to draw your attention toward him.

You may notice he'll touch his face a lot .. This is an unconscious gesture for you to notice how attractive he is.

Men don't realize they are doing these things, they are just what happens and they are a way for you to understand what he's saying, without embarrassing or making a fool of yourself.

Masculinity: The Macho Pose

It's innate in men to want to show you how masculine they are ... so they do what they can to show their prowess by doing the macho pose, which is to stand tall, square their shoulder, and put their hands on the waist, kind of like superman when he's not flying around saving people.

I am in Control

A typical male needs to be in control and show you he is the boss. Before a man closes a distance between himself and the other person involved, he may at first stand a little farther away in order to make observations about the situation. Once he has assessed the situation, and feels he's in control, he will move in closer. Men typically tend to lean back when listening, except when the person is a woman he is attracted to.

The Body Language Of Women

Women send body language signals five times stronger than men. You will see that the female body language is easy to read.

How To Read The Female Body Language

Women are very expressive, but they can give mixed signals if you are trying to read them the same way you read a man. So, in women it's best to look for several signals. For example, you cannot tell if a woman is into you merely by eye contact alone. Women typically give good eye contact in conversations with everything. But, if she is smiling, fiddling with her clothes, if her eyes are very dilated ... these are great signs. Again, with women, the key is to find signs that are layered.

A few other gestures her body will make are that her shoulders will be completely parallel with your shoulders, facing you.

Her toes will be pointed either shoulder width apart or if crossed the toe will be pointing toward you.

Is She Flirting?

The most typical signal that a woman is flirting with you is the way in which she interacts with her personal appearance. She will always like to look her best for you. So, she'll play with her hair, by twirling with her finger into a few swirls, she's swing her hair around or toss it over her shoulder. She'll try to expose a little skin, accidentally on purpose.

If you are across the room from her, you will know that she is into you as well if she keeps glancing over. The eye contact she makes is usually longer than usual and then would look down with a flattered or embarrassed smile.

Women also do a good job in catching their men's attention with movements of their lips. A strong lip flirting signal is when she would bite or lick her lips. You may notice she is careful about they way in, which she takes a drink from a glass or eats in a slow motion. This is done to bring lots of attention to the lips.

But the best sign of flirting is when she laughs at your jokes. Did you really think you were that funny? Take it as a compliment. If she is laughing she is probably very interested.

If she touches you more than one time, this is a great sign. Women may even create a false reason for touching you, such as accidently brushing up against you, or bending over to pick something up to get your attention.

She's Saying Yes

It is a definite signal of invitation when she keeps looking back at you. A smile would strengthen the signal of attraction. You will know she is interested in your interaction if she keeps that eye contact even if she's playing with something with her hand, or her jewelry or her drinking glass or her hair. There is a certain glow in a woman's eyes and facial expression when she likes a particular person. Another sign is when she would step closer to you or touch you.

She's Saying No

The strongest sign that a woman is annoyed, uninterested, and bothered by you is the arms crossed. Some women are kind enough to be just civil, especially during a blind date with the wrong guy. But, observe her eyes. See if the glow is there or if they are dull and unexpressive. Notice if the smile happens on the entire face, or if it's forced and only the mouth is smiling, but not the eyes. If there is eye contact, and she's not into you, she keeps breaking it and tries to avoid making eye contact.

Female body language is not that difficult to read, especially once you get to know a woman better and practice watching and working with how her body reacts to you.

Chapter 7: Body Language For A Job Interview

A job interview is a very first and one of the most important steps toward gaining employment. They key to success in getting hired for that special job does not only depend on the documents you have submitted. Your potential employer is going to consider how you are, in your ability to demonstrate confidence in your skills and doing the job. Knowingly or unknowingly, that employer is going to be studying your body language.

Be Conscious Of Your Actions

Be aware of how your body moves or acts.

A job interview is very essential for both the employer and applicant for the very reason that it will be the basis of finalizing the decision about the applicant for the vacant job. Thus, as the applicant, it is relevant that he or she must be fully prepared for the job interview. You must remember that the employer or interviewer does not only consider the way you dress, your credentials, or even your answers to his questions. Your body language is also being observed.

Your body language can tell another person what kind of person you are, your emotions, and your state of mind. An employer would be looking for a confident and competent employee. Thus, you should know and learn the posture to maintain, movements to impress, and gestures to avoid during the interview.

If You Want To Show Interest

To show signs of interest, be sure to have plenty of eye contact and maintain it. Eye Contact is a definite sign of giving your attention to that person. Frequent nodding and leaning your body towards that person also indicates that you are listening to him or her.

Posture And Body Movements

Your interview is usually going to begin with a good firm handshake. Be sure to look the interviewer in the eyes and smile. Your palm should be able to touch the palm of your interviewer. Extend your arm and point your hand downwards. This is going to immediately get you into a good feeling of confidence and rapport with each other.

Let the interviewer run the show. Be seated when and where they ask you. A good posture for interviewing is one that is relaxed, yet the back remains straight with your chin slightly held up and your shoulders pulled back. Do not sit at the edge of the chair, this would mean that you are too nervous or tense. Simply relax into your chair, and place your hands on your lap. Crossing the legs is not really advisable, but nonetheless it is fine, as long as the direction of your body is towards the interviewer.

This posture demonstrates confidence, which by now you should realize is something employers like to see.

Having good posture actually causes people will treat you differently. They will treat you with more respect.

Movements To Impress

When responding, make use of your hands. Showing your palm when explaining something indicates that you are being relaxed, honest, and confident. The interviewer will think that you know what you are talking about. If you want to emphasize something, you can do it with a clenched fist; but this is not an advisable gesture during an interview.

You can show interest and that you are listening attentively to your interviewer through head movements. Nodding is a reinforcement that you understood or agreed to what he or she said. Even though there are ideas that you would like to oppose to, nodding is still preferable rather than arguing. The latter might be the reason why you cannot get the job.

Gestures to Avoid

One must avoid slouching, which indicates laziness and boredom. Do not tighten your body muscle either; this will make you look stiff thus making you look nervous and lacking confidence. Or it can give your interviewer that you may be hiding something from him, or you are uninterested to get the job Do not place your hands into your pockets; this reflects your anxiety and discomfort. Lack of confidence is very well reflected in tapping of the foot, drumming of the fingers, and fidgeting.

You can use hand movements when talking, however do not overuse them. Excess movements can be distracting.

There are many gestures that are regarded as rude by most people, or that you are avoiding to interact with them. This includes crossing the arms across the chest, holding objects such as books and a bag in front of you, inspecting the time on your watch or the clock, stroking your chin, standing too close, staring or narrowing your eyes, forcing smiles, placing the hand on the waist, touching your face frequently, blinking more than usual, foot tapping, and many more. Most of these gestures are done unconsciously, but nonetheless, the people who you are talking to may be offended by those actions.

Another gesture you must avoid is frequent eye movement. Avoiding the interviewer's eyes will make him think that you are not listening or getting bored and uninterested.

Chapter 8: Conclusion

Every part of ones body is used in body language, each movement or lack of movement can mean something. Not everyone exhibits the exact same body language as another to express something, such as in greetings, for one it may be customary to kiss another on both sides of the cheek, but for another a simple wave of the hand suffices.

Some people use less emphasis with their body language where others can over exaggerate the same gesture. Some people require larger personal space where others are quite comfortable with others moving in close. There are so many different facets to body language, and one can never stop learning. By watching people, I am sure you will even be able to pick up more signs of body language being used then the brief introduction I have given you here.

Learning and knowing how to read body language will help you in all aspects of your life. Take the time to read a body today.

I wish you success!

Made in the USA
San Bernardino, CA
19 January 2017